ON THE COVER
Herbert Hoover birthplace cottage at Herbert Hoover NHS, prescribed fire at Tallgrass Prairie NPres, aquatic invertebrate monitoring at George Washington Carver NM, the Mississippi River at Effigy Mounds NM.

An Evaluation of Biological Inventory Data Collected at Pipestone National Monument

Vertebrate and Vascular Plant Inventories

Natural Resource Technical Report NPS/HTLN/NRTR—2009/249

Michael H. Williams
Kodge Data Services
150 Shady Branch
Benton, MO 63736

October 2009

U.S. Department of the Interior
National Park Service
Natural Resource Program Center
Fort Collins, Colorado

The National Park Service, Natural Resource Program Center publishes a range of reports that address natural resource topics of interest and applicability to a broad audience in the National Park Service and others in natural resource management, including scientists, conservation and environmental constituencies, and the public.

The Natural Resource Technical Report Series is used to disseminate results of scientific studies in the physical, biological, and social sciences for both the advancement of science and the achievement of the National Park Service mission. The series provides contributors with a forum for displaying comprehensive data that are often deleted from journals because of page limitations.

All manuscripts in the series receive the appropriate level of peer review to ensure that the information is scientifically credible, technically accurate, appropriately written for the intended audience, and designed and published in a professional manner. This report received informal peer review by subject-matter experts who were not directly involved in the collection, analysis, or reporting of the data.

Views, statements, findings, conclusions, recommendations, and data in this report are those of the author(s) and do not necessarily reflect views and policies of the National Park Service, U.S. Department of the Interior. Mention of trade names or commercial products does not constitute endorsement or recommendation for use by the National Park Service.

This report is available from http://science.nature.nps.gov/im/units/htln/ and the Natural Resource Publications Management website (http://www.nature.nps.gov/publications/NRPM/).

Please cite this publication as:

Williams, M. H. 2009. An evaluation of biological inventory data collected at Pipestone National Monument: Vertebrate and vascular plant inventories. Natural Resource Technical Report NPS/HTLN/NRTR—2009/249. National Park Service, Fort Collins, Colorado.

NPS XXXXXX, Month Year

Contents

Tables

Abstract

The Inventory and Monitoring program of the NPS provides twelve basic inventories for park managers, including lists of species that occur in NPS units. Eight hundred seventy two species are certified on the list of vascular plants and vertebrates for Pipestone National Monument (PIPE). Based on a review of the evidence, 715 (82%) species were categorized as Present in Park, and 157 (18%) as Probably Present. Seventy three species were Unconfirmed. In addition to documenting the presence of species, reviewers categorized the general abundance of 567 (79%) species and determined residency for all documented vertebrates with the exception of 90 (1 amphibian, 2 mammals, 87 birds). Species lists for PIPE can be queried from the Natural Resource Information Portal at http://nrinfo.nps.gov/Home.mvc.

Eighty three non-native species are documented to occur in the park. Of these are four birds, one fish, one mammal, and 77 vascular plants. Non-native vascular plant species were assigned a NatureServe Invasive Species Impact Rank (I-Rank) based on impact to native species and natural biodiversity. Thirteen of the 77 (17%) non-native plants found on PIPE received an overall I-Rank score that included the high category (i.e. most threatening).

A total of 42 species are listed by the Minnesota Department of Natural Resources as a species of conservation status. The federally listed threatened western prairie fringed orchid and endangered Topeka shiner are documented on PIPE. The federally listed threatened piping plover is noted as probably present. Sixteen state listed species include three threatened species documented on PIPE (mud plantain, short pointed umbrella sedge, slender plantain) and six listed as probably present (common tern, horned grebe, loggerhead shrike, peregrine falcon, Wilson's phalarope, Blanding's turtle). Three state listed endangered species were documented on PIPE (Henslow's sparrow, blackfoot quillwort, hairy water clover) and two (king rail, Sprague's pipit) were listed as probably present. Two additional endangered species noted as unconfirmed include the burrowing owl and chestnut collared longspur. Future inventory efforts are discussed.

Acknowledgements

Thanks go to the inventory project researchers and their many volunteers including: Dan Fogell, University of Nebraska, Omaha, NE. Additional thanks go to NPS personnel including Park, Heartland Network, Midwest Region, and Washington Office staff. A special thanks to the staff of Pipestone National Monument for allowing access to the park during inventory and monitoring efforts.

Introduction

As part of the National Park Service's effort to "improve park management through greater reliance on scientific knowledge," a primary role of the Inventory and Monitoring (I&M) Program is to collect, organize, and make available natural resource data. A list of species known to occur in NPS units is considered a basic inventory need (see: http://science.nature.nps.gov/im/inventory/index.cfm). The I&M Program's Heartland Network (HTLN) recently completed inventories of vertebrate species and vascular plants at Pipestone National Monument (PIPE). In doing so, all existing data were cataloged, targeted field investigations were conducted, and species lists were certified by taxonomic experts. The primary goal of these efforts was to document at least 90% of the vertebrate and vascular plant species believed to occur in the park. This report provides a summary of results.

Methods

The HTLN followed a strategic plan of action set forth in an Inventory Study Plan (Boetsch et al. 2000) to complete inventories of vascular plants and vertebrate species. This plan was instigated by the Natural Resource Challenge in response to the National Parks Omnibus Management Act of 1998 and adheres to the requisite approaches delineated in Guidelines for Biological Inventories (NPS 1999) and the recommendations of the Service-wide I&M Program. The Inventory Study Plan identified steps to conduct a natural resource "information assessment" of existing park data. These steps included (1) developing master lists of species known or expected to occur in the park, (2) conducting field inventories, and (3) certifying the resultant species data.

> The term species (as opposed to organism) is generically used throughout this report to refer to unique taxa at the species level or below.

Expected Species Lists

In order to determine the completeness of inventory information, the HTLN developed lists of vascular plants and vertebrates expected to occur in the park. The master lists of fish was derived from fish surveys conducted in and around PIPE by Konrad Schmidt (1989) and from stocking data supplied by the Minnesota Department of Natural Resources. The master lists of birds were derived from range maps in The Golden Guide, A Guide To Field Identification Of North American Birds (Robbins et al. 1983), and National Geographic Society's Field Guide To The Birds Of North America (1987). Expected amphibians were derived from the U.S. amphibian distribution map internet site at http://home.bsu.edu/~00MJLANNOO/USamphibians.html. The range maps of Conant and Collins (1998) "A Field Guide to Reptiles and Amphibians of Eastern and Central North America" (need reference for Literature cited section) were used to derive expected reptile species lists. Any problems associated with synonymy were resolved by following Conant and Collins (1998). Gunderson and Beer's (1953) Mammals of Minnesota was used to develop the mammal list. An initial compilation and evaluation of park floras was completed by Dr. Jim Bennett, National Wildlife Health Center, USGS BRD (Bennett 1995). Bennett compiled floras from "numerous sources: park lists, published journal articles and books, vegetation surveys, natural history reports, herbarium lists, park files and memoranda, and other miscellaneous park reports." Species names were standardized to USDA PLANTS (1999) and inconsistencies in infraspecific designations were resolved on a case-by-case basis.

Compiling Existing Inventory Data

Concurrent with development of expected species lists, HTLN staff worked with technical support from the Natural Resource Program Center (NRPC) to consolidate existing inventories. HTLN staff searched for existing inventory data, extracted species lists from the reports, labeled the lists with appropriate reference information, and forwarded the data to NRPC for processing.

HTLN staff mined inventory data from regional inventory databases, and transferred the network's Flora database. Staff also assembled bibliographic data concerning the primary park inventories. The Procite bibliographic database, NatureBib (aka NRBIB), was queried to produce an initial list of references. The lists were reviewed to ensure that each inventory: 1) included primary, rather than secondary, inventory data; 2) was based on observed, not expected, occurrences; and 3) was the result of professional surveys or research, rather than amateur observations. Park resource managers then reviewed and added to the lists.

HTLN staff searched for references to botanical collections as sources of species occurrence records. The process of searching regional herbaria for pertinent species records then commenced. The primary objectives were: 1) to find previously unknown collections; and 2) to document the current repository for older, known collections. The HTLN initiated a cooperative agreement with the National Wildlife Health Center (Biological Resources Division) to conduct computerized searches of regional and national museums and herbaria for park records of vertebrate and vascular plant occurrences. Given the limited timeframe, repositories with searchable collections databases were used. Dr. Jim Bennett, author of a summary of Midwestern NPS floras (Bennett 1995), was the principal investigator and was assisted with results of a search of the PIPE ANCS+ database collection provided by the HTLN.

> ANCS+ is a database management system developed by NPS to accession and catalog its museum collections.

The NPSpecies Database

NPSpecies is a master database for documenting the occurrence and status of all organisms in NPS units. The database includes standardized information associated with the occurrence of species, including scientific names and their synonyms (i.e. a local list or a standard list of species names), common names, abundance, residency, nativity, T&E status, and notes of particular management interest to a park. NPSpecies supports NPS staff and collaborators at the park, network, regional, and national levels by managing fundamental park-level species information, and making this information available to other applications and databases for more specialized analyses. A primary purpose for NPSpecies is to provide park managers, planners, and scientists with basic information on species occurrences and status for making decisions and working with other agencies, the scientific community, and the public for the long-term protection of park ecosystems (NPSpecies 2009).

Within NPSpecies, each species record is supported by evidence in the form of voucher specimens, references (scientific reports or datasets), and/or observation records that document the occurrence of the species in the park. Historical and currently-accepted scientific names from multiple taxonomic classification systems are cross-referenced using taxonomic standards (e.g., the Integrated Taxonomic Information System and the USDA PLANTS database) to allow for data integration and sharing across parks and with other agencies and organizations. In addition, parks are able to produce species lists based on the taxonomic authorities that are most accepted in their region and by their partner agencies.

Populating NPSpecies focused on three objectives: 1) transferring existing data; 2) including evidence for each record; and 3) verifying the accuracy of lists. As master species lists were compiled and transferred into NPSpecies a conservative approach was taken while assigning park status (e.g. present, probably present, etc.) to ensure that assessments of completeness were based on verifiable records. Many records imported from previous databases were unsubstantiated (i.e. not linked to a verifiable data source) and were classified as unconfirmed. Verification of vertebrate taxa was conducted by comparing digital records to original sources. The process proved valuable for assuring data quality as transcription errors, spelling mistakes, erroneous names, and synonymy problems were identified and corrected. In the process, park status (e.g. present in park, probable, unconfirmed) were also updated. After verifying and

3

updating, any remaining species without evidence were assigned an 'unconfirmed' status. Reliable status information is necessary to generate verifiable species lists for use in assessing inventory completeness. WASO I&M then completed the processing of these data and returned an NPSpecies database.

Inventories

Targeted field inventories were conducted to augment existing inventory data while addressing information gaps and high priority information needs. Two workshops were held during FY 2000 to assist in determining and prioritizing inventory needs (see appendix F in Boetsch et al. 2000). Regional taxa experts participated in these workshops and helped to revise project plans and priorities, and develop a greater awareness of taxa-specific inventory methods.

Subsequent to these initial steps, the HTLN began implementing inventories of amphibians and reptiles, birds, fish, mammals, and vascular plants. When completed, inventory reports were submitted to the HTLN and, once finalized, bibliographic data and the final report were uploaded to NatureBib. Species data (ie. taxonomic name, park status, abundance, etc.) and voucher data were uploaded to NPSpecies. Primary inventory data (ie. locations, events, etc.) and inventory specific data (i.e. bird counts, amphibian observations, etc.) were entered in a Microsoft (MS) Access database standardized to the current natural resource database template (NRDT) and uploaded to the NPS Data Store.

Inventory Certification

To support the objective of documenting 90% of vertebrate and vascular plant species expected to occur, subject matter experts (i.e. those involved with PIPE inventories) participated in the NPSpecies certification of taxonomic and attribute data for each taxa list. The process of certification is a data validation and quality assurance procedure for species checklists performed by subject matter experts most familiar with a particular taxonomic category. Taxon nomenclature are documented as well as park status, abundance, residency, and nativity.

Amphibian and reptile certifications were compiled with current inventory data (Fogell 2003). Bird, fish, mammal, and vascular plant certifications were conducted by PIPE and HTLN staff. Generally, species lists were distributed as MS Excel worksheets and returned with revisions. Revised expected species lists containing a species park status (present, probably present, etc), abundance (common, uncommon, rare, etc), residency (breeder, resident, etc), and nativity as well as other attribute details were then updated (where necessary) via the desktop NPSpecies to reflect the current species' park status. These lists were then uploaded to the master online version of NPSpecies.

Results

Fifteen references (see Appendix 1) and 16 vouchers led to the certification of 872 species (NPSpecies 2009). In total, 715 species were categorized as Present in Park and 157 as Probably Present (Table 1). Additionally, 73 species were categorized as Unconfirmed. Unconfirmed species were ranked as such due to weak evidence supporting their existence on the park.

Currently 76% of the species on the park's species list are documented (i.e., categorized as Present in Park). If species listed as Present in Park and Probably Present are included in the calculation, the percentage of documented species rises to 92%.

Table 1. Count of species by park status categories at PIPE (NPSpecies 2009).

Park Status[1]	Bird	Fish	Mammal	Amphibian	Reptile	Vascular Plant	Total
Present in Park	110	18	21	6	3	557	715
Probably Present	142	2	10		3		157
Encroaching							
Unconfirmed	68		1		2	2	73
Historic							
Total	320	20	32	6	8	559	945

[1] Refer to the Appendix for definitions of Park Status categories.

Of the 715 species documented as present, reviewers assigned a general abundance category (e.g., common, rare, etc.) to 567 (79%) (Table 2). Reviewers believed additional information was needed before an abundance category could be assigned to the remaining 148 (21%) species. Results are available to NPS staff through the Natural Resource Information Portal at http://nrinfo.nps.gov/Home.mvc. The portal is the product of the Integration of Resource Management Applications (IRMA) project. To learn more see: http://www1.nrintra.nps.gov/im/datamgmt/docs/IRMA_ProjectBrief_v1.0.pdf.

Residency values (e.g., breeder, migrant, resident, etc.) were assigned for all documented vertebrates with the exception of 90 that were categorized as unknown (1 amphibian, 2 mammals, and 87 birds). Unknown residency values were assigned primarily because it was unclear as to whether or not the species bred on the park. Non-natives documented to occur in the park (i.e., Present in Park) total 83. Of these are four birds, one fish, one mammal, and 77 vascular plants.

NatureServe, in cooperation with The Nature Conservancy and NPS, developed a protocol to rank the impact of non-native invasive vascular plants (Morse et al. 2004). Through a series of standardized questions, non-native species are evaluated and assigned an Invasive Species Impact Rank (I-Rank) based on impact to native species and natural biodiversity. I-Ranks are categorized as high, medium, low, or insignificant. Thirteen of the 77 (17%) non-native plants found on PIPE received an overall I-Rank score that included the high category (Table 3). All are known to occur in the park (i.e., Present in Park).

A total of 42 species (Table 4) are listed by the Minnesota Department of Natural Resources as a species of conservation status. Additional NatureServe global, national, and subnational ranking status is provided. The federally listed threatened western prairie fringed orchid (*Platanthera praeclara*) and endangered Topeka shiner (*Notropis topeka*) are documented on PIPE. The federally listed threatened piping plover (*Charadrius melodus*) is noted as probably present. Sixteen state listed species include three threatened species documented on PIPE (mud plantain, *Heteranthera limosa*, short pointed umbrella sedge, *Cyperus acuminatus*, slender plantain, *Plantago elongata*) and six noted as probably present (common tern, *Sterna hirundo*, horned grebe, *Podiceps auritus*, loggerhead shrike, *Lanius ludovicianus*, peregrine falcon, *Falco peregrinus*, Wilson's phalarope, *Phalaropus tricolor*, Blanding's turtle, *Emydoidea blandingii*). Three state listed endangered species were documented on PIPE (Henslow's sparrow, *Ammodramus henslowii*, blackfoot quillwort, *Isoetes melanopoda*, hairy water clover, *Marsilea vestita*) and two noted as probably present (king rail, *Rallus elegans*, Sprague's pipit, *Anthus spragueii*). Two additional endangered species noted as unconfirmed include the burrowing owl (*Athene cunicularia*) and chestnut collared longspur (*Calcarius ornatus*).

Table 2. Count of species by abundance categories at PIPE (NPSpecies 2009).

Abundance Category[1]	Bird	Fish	Mammal	Amphibian	Reptile	Vascular Plant	Total
Abundant			2				2
Common			6			4	10
Uncommon			2			538	540
Rare			2			13	15
Occasional							
Unknown	110	18	9	6	3	2	148
Total	110	18	21	6	3	557	715

[1] Refer to the Appendix for definitions of Park Status categories.

7

Table 3. Non-native plants, occurring on PIPE, with an Invasive Species Impact Rank (I-Rank) containing high.

Scientific Name	Common Name	Overall I-Rank	Ecological Impact[1]	Management Difficulty[2]	I-Rank Reasons Summary[3]
Bromus tectorum	Cheatgrass	High	High	High / Medium	Found in all fifty states; widespread in abandoned fields, riparian vegetation, riparian meadows, grasslands, abandoned cropland, roadsides, and "waste places".
Campanula rapunculoides	Creeping bellflower	High / Low	Medium / Low	High / Low	Established in most states in the continental U.S. except California, Arizona, and the southeast; vigorous, persistent herbaceous perennial that spreads by deep-seated creeping roots.
Carduus nutans	Nodding thistle	High / Low	Medium / Insignificant	High / Medium	Persistent in open areas, including prairies, grasslands, roadsides and areas of disturbance in dense woods; prolific seed production; seeds viable for up to 15 years.
Cirsium arvense	Creeping thistle	High / Medium	Medium / Low	High / Medium	Widespread, well recognized non-native that is on the majority of states' noxious species lists.
Coronilla varia	Crown vetch	High	High	Low	This perennial herb is a nitrogen-fixer, alters the fuel loads in fire-adapted ecosystems, creates dense monospecific stands by strongly out-competing native plants, and impacts the high-quality occurrence of common and rare native plant communities in the U.S.
Elaeagnus angustifolia	Russian olive	High	High / Medium	High	Very aggressive in western U.S.; primarily invading riparian areas, it is also found in open areas from grasslands to sparse woodlands.
Elymus repens	Creeping wild rye	High / Medium	Medium / Low	High / Medium	Widespread occurring in nearly every U.S. state; negative impacts are significant as this species has the potential to form dense, monospecific stands.

8

Table 3 (cont.). Non-native plants, occurring on PIPE, with an Invasive Species Impact Rank (I-Rank) containing high.

Scientific Name	Common Name	Overall I-Rank	Ecological Impact[1]	Management Difficulty[2]	I-Rank Reasons Summary[3]
Euphorbia esula	Leafy spurge	High / Medium	Medium	High	Considered to be a pest because of the speed that it invaded (and continues to invade) as well as the extreme difficulty to control and manage the infestation.
Linaria vulgaris	Butter and eggs	High / Low	Medium / Low	High / Medium	An aggressive invader in many parts of the U.S.
Lonicera tatarica	Tatarian honeysuckle	High / Medium	Medium	Medium	Exhibits some canopy disturbance reducing species richness and abundance and inhibiting native tree seedlings. Negative impacts on community composition.
Phalaris arundinacea	Reed canarygrass	High	High	High / Medium	This species can form dense, persistent, monotypic stands of creeping rhizomes in a thick sod layer in wetlands, moist meadows and riparian areas.
Poa compressa	Canada bluegrass	High / Low	Medium / Low	High / Medium	Widespread in the U.S. in disturbed areas, prairies, and ridgetop woodlands; may crowd out native species; forms large colonies; spreads very quickly; control is difficult.
Rhamnus cathartica	Common buckthorn	High / Medium	Medium	Medium	Widespread across the continental U.S.; can form even-aged, dense thickets shading out natives and often obliterating them; suppresses fire in fire-adapted communities.

[1] Subcategory of Overall I-Rank specifically addressing species negative impacts on native plant/animal populations/communities.
[2] Subcategory of Overall I-Rank specifically addressing difficulty of control.
[3] Summary reasons for NatureServe Overall I-Rank. For more information see the NatureServe Species Explorer at http://www.natureserve.org. These summaries reflective of NatureServe data last updated 6 February, 2009.

Table 4. Species on the park's local list which possess a state heritage program rank and/or other designated conservation status (State Heritage Conservation Rank/Status, Global, National, Subnational, and/or a Federal Status).

Bird	Scientific Name	Park Status[1]	State Heritage Program Status[2]	Federal Status[3]	Global / National / Subnational Status[4]	Global Short Term Trend[4]
Acadian flycatcher	Empidonax virescens	Unconfirmed	Special Concern		G5 / N5B / S3B	Increasing
American white pelican	Pelecanus erythrorhynchos	Unconfirmed	Special Concern		G4 / N4 / S3B	Increasing
Bald eagle	Haliaeetus leucocephalus	Probably Present	Special Concern		G5 / N5B,N5N / S3B,S3N	Stable to increasing
Burrowing owl	Athene cunicularia	Unconfirmed	Endangered		G4 / N4B,N4N / S1B	Declining
Cerulean warbler	Dendroica cerulea	Probably Present	Special Concern		G4 / N4B / S3B	Declining (decline of 10-30%)
Chestnut collared longspur	Calcarius ornatus	Unconfirmed	Endangered		G5 / N5B,N5N / S1B	Declining
Common moorhen	Gallinula chloropus	Probably Present	Special Concern		G5 / N5B,N5N / S3B	Local declines
Common tern	Sterna hirundo	Probably Present	Threatened		G5 / N5B / S2B	
Forster's tern	Sterna forsteri	Probably Present	Special Concern		G5 / N5B,N5N / S3B	
Franklin's gull	Larus pipixcan	Present in Park	Special Concern		G4 / N4B / S3B	
Greater prairie-chicken	Tympanuchus cupido	Unconfirmed	Special Concern		G4 / N4 / S3	
Henslow's sparrow	Ammodramus henslowii	Present in Park	Endangered		G4 / N3B,N4N / S1B	Severely declining
Hooded warbler	Wilsonia citrina	Unconfirmed	Special Concern		G5 / N5B / S3B	Increasing
Horned grebe	Podiceps auritus	Probably Present	Threatened		G5 / N5B,N5N / S2B	
King rail	Rallus elegans	Probably Present	Endangered		G4 / N4B,N4N / S1B	Rapidly declining to declining
Loggerhead shrike	Lanius ludovicianus	Probably Present	Threatened		G4 / N4 / S2B	Rapidly declining to declining

Table 4 (cont.). Species on the park's local list which possess a state heritage program rank and/or other designated conservation status (State Heritage Conservation Rank/Status, Global, National, Subnational, and/or a Federal Status).

Bird	Scientific Name	Park Status[1]	State Heritage Program Status[2]	Federal Status[3]	Global / National / Subnational Status[4]	Global Short Term Trend[4]
Louisiana waterthrush	Seiurus motacilla	Unconfirmed	Special Concern		G5 / N5B / S3B	Stable
Marbled godwit	Limosa fedoa	Probably Present	Special Concern		G5 / N5B,N5N / S3B	
Peregrine falcon	Falco peregrinus	Probably Present	Threatened		G4 / N4B,N4N / S2B	Increasing
Piping plover	Charadrius melodus	Probably Present	Endangered	Threatened	G3 / N3B,N3N / S1B	Stable
Red-shouldered hawk	Buteo lineatus	Unconfirmed	Special Concern		G5 / N5B,N5N / S3B,SNRN	Stable to increasing
Short eared owl	Asio flammeus	Probably Present	Special Concern		G5 / N5B,N5N / S3B	Declining (decline of 10-30%)
Sprague's pipit	Anthus spragueii	Probably Present	Endangered		G4 / N4B,N4N / S1B	Declining (decline of 10-30%)
Wilson's phalarope	Phalaropus tricolor	Probably Present	Threatened		G5 / N5B / S2B	Declining (decline of 10-30%)
Yellow rail	Coturnicops noveboracensis	Probably Present	Special Concern		G4 / N3B,N4N / S3B	Declining (decline of 10-30%)
Fish						
Topeka shiner	Notropis topeka	Present in Park	Special Concern	Endangered	G3 / N3 / S3	Declining to Stable
Mammal						
Least weasel	Mustela nivalis	Present in Park	Special Concern		G5 / N5 / S3	
Reptile						
Blanding's turtle	Emydoidea blandingii	Probably Present	Threatened		G4 / N4 / S2	Declining to stable
Lined snake	Tropidoclonion lineatum	Unconfirmed	Special Concern		G5 / N5 / S3	Stable

Table 4 (cont.). Species on the park's local list which possess a state heritage program rank and/or other designated conservation status (State Heritage Conservation Rank/Status, Global, National, Subnational, and/or a Federal Status).

	Scientific Name	Park Status[1]	State Heritage Program Status[2]	Federal Status[3]	Global / National / Subnational Status[4]	Global Short Term Trend[4]
Reptile						
Snapping turtle	*Chelydra serpentina*	Present in Park	Special Concern		G5 / N5 / S3	Stable
Vascular Plant						
Blackfoot quillwort	*Isoetes melanopoda*	Present in Park	Endangered		G5 / N5 / S1	
Buffalo grass	*Buchloe dactyloides*	Present in Park	Special Concern		G4 / N4N5 / S3	
Coralberry	*Symphoricarpos orbiculatus*	Present in Park	Special Concern		G5 / N5? / SNA	
Hairy water clover	*Marsilea vestita*	Present in Park	Endangered		G5 / N5? / S1	
Mud plantain	*Heteranthera limosa*	Present in Park	Threatened		G5 / N4N5 / S2	
Mudwort	*Limosella aquatica*	Present in Park	Special Concern		G5 / NNR / S3	
Plains prickly pear	*Opuntia macrorhiza*	Present in Park	Special Concern		G5 / N5 / S3	
Short-pointed umbrella-sedge	*Cyperus acuminatus*	Present in Park	Threatened		G5 / N5 / S2	
Slender plantain	*Plantago elongata*	Present in Park	Threatened		G4 / N4 / S2	
Tumblegrass	*Schedonnardus paniculatus*	Present in Park	Special Concern		G5 / N3N5 / S3	
Water-hyssop	*Bacopa rotundifolia*	Present in Park	Special Concern		G5 / NNR / S3	
Western prairie fringed orchid	*Platanthera praeclara*	Present in Park	Endangered	Threatened	G3 / N3 / S1	Declining (decline of 10-30%)

[1] Refer to the Appendix for definitions of Park Status categories.
[2] The official endangerment status the Minnesota Department of Natural Resources has assigned to this species. (http://files.dnr.state.mn.us/natural_resources/ets/endlist.pdf).

3 U.S. Endangered Species Act: Current status of the taxon as designated or proposed by the U.S. Fish and Wildlife Service (USFWS), and as reported in the U.S. Federal Register in accordance with the U.S. Endangered Species Act of 1973, as amended.

4 The NatureServe conservation status, developed by NatureServe and its network of member (state) programs, of a species from a state/province perspective, characterizing the relative imperilment of the species. G = global (rounded), N = national, and S = subnational; 1 = critically imperiled, 2 = imperiled, 3 = vulnerable, 4 = apparently secure, 5 = secure; B=Breeding population, NR=Not rated. Refer to http://www.natureserve.org/explorer/ranking.htm#interpret for additional information on conservation status ranks.

Discussion

The NPS Inventory Strategic Plan states that "the ultimate goal is to establish an accurate inventory of all life forms within a park..." (NPS 2009, see also NPS 1992). The HTLN supports this goal by documenting over 80% of all vertebrates and vascular plants known to occur at PIPE. One result of these efforts is the compilation of reliable species lists. These lists, however sound, should always be considered incomplete. Inventory lists will change as new information about species distributions becomes available. The overall number of species designated as Present in Park or Probably Present is similar to similarly sized parks in the HTLN (Table 5).

Table 5. Number of species designated as present in park or probably present in HTLN parks (NPSpecies 2009).

Park	Bird	Fish	Mammal	Amphibian	Reptile	Vascular Plants	TOTALS	Park Size (ac.)
PIPE	252	20	31	6	6	557	872	282
HOME	81	31	41	6	9	304	472	160
HEHO	120	28	45	1	11	230	435	186
LIBO	224	-	38	13	13	332	620	200
GWCA	192	34	44	8	17	662	957	210
HOCU	274	15	40	21	25	457	832	280
ARPO	111	65	33	17	40	332	598	389
EFMO	220	93	43	9	21	426	812	1,481
WICR	134	53	48	11	31	569	846	1,750
PERI	74	41	44	21	36	665	881	4,300
HOSP	114	52	49	22	45	910	1,192	5,549
TAPR	136	29	42	8	27	456	698	10,894
CUVA	241	65	37	19	21	1,167	1,550	32,859
OZAR	167	122	55	29	45	880	1,298	82,196
BUFF	211	78	58	22	43	1,353	1,765	95,730

Future Inventory Efforts

While significant strides have been made in documenting the presence of vertebrate species and vascular plants, it is anticipated that additional survey efforts will be required to increase the number of documented species (i.e. Present in Park). For example, more than half of the birds and half the mammals and reptiles are listed as probably present or unconfirmed and lack adequate documentation. Additionally, several state listed species are listed as probably present or unconfirmed. If species are thought to be Probably Present or Unconfirmed, follow-up surveys (perhaps targeted inventories?) are warranted or existing monitoring programs broadened to include searches for these species. Additional follow up inventories coupled with habitat studies may document their presence.

Reviewers assigned a general abundance category for all but 148 of the documented species (six amphibians, 110 birds, 18 fish, nine mammals, three reptiles, and two

14

vascular plants). Reviewers also assigned a residency value for all but 90. Continued monitoring of the species may provide for updated abundance and residency.

Based on the results of the data reported herein, future inventory recommendations include:

- additional resources to survey for species listed in Table 4,
- coupled with the above, focus on species listed as Probably Present, Unconfirmed, and Historic,

Key Findings of Management Interest

- The recent herpetofauna inventory (Fogell 2003) documented a relatively low diversity of amphibians and reptiles. Only five of nine species of amphibians and four of nine species of reptiles were encountered. Several species of exotic and/or invasive plants were noted that may have a potentially harmful affect on the ecosystem at PIPE. These include dame's rocket (*Hesperis matronalis*) and leafy spurge (*Euphorbia esula*).

Literature Cited

Bennett, J. P. 1995. Floristic summary of 22 Midwestern national parks. Wisconsin Cooperative Park Studies Unit, USGS, BRD.

Boetsch, J., M. DeBacker, P. Hughes, D. Peitz, L. Thomas, G. Wagner, and B. Witcher. 2000. A study plan to inventory vascular plants and vertebrates: HTLN NPS.

Conant, R. and J. T. Collins. 1998. Reptiles and amphibians: eastern/central North America. Houghton Mifflin. Boston, Massachusetts.

Fogell, D. 2003. A herpetofaunal inventory of Tallgrass Prairie National Preserve, Homestead National Monument of America, and Pipestone National Monument within the Heartland Inventory and Monitoring Network. National Park Service.

Gunderson, H.L. and J.R. Beer. 1953. The mammals of Minnesota. Mus. of Natur. Hist., Univ. of Minnesota, Minneapolis, Occas. Paper no. 6. 190 pp.

Morse, L. E., J. M. Randall, N. Benton, R. Hiebert, and S. Lu. 2004. An invasive species assessment protocol: Evaluating non-native plants for their impact on biodiversity. Version 1. NatureServe, Arlington, Virginia.

National Geographic Society. 1987. Field guide to the birds of North America. Washington, D.C. National Geographic Society. 464 p.

National Park Service. 1992. NPS-75: Natural resources inventory and monitoring guideline. National Park Service, Inventory and Monitoring Program.

National Park Service. 1999. Guidelines for biological inventories. Inventory and Monitoring Program, National Park Service. 10 pp.

National Park Service. 2009. Strategic plan for natural resource inventories, FY 2008 – FY 2012. Natural Resource Report NPS/NRPC/NRR—2009/094. National Park Service, Fort Collins, Colorado.

NPSpecies Proper: NPSpecies - The National Park Service biodiversity database. Secure online version. https://science1.nature.nps.gov/npspecies/web/main/start. Accessed May, 2009.

Robbins, C. S., Bruun, B., and H. S. Zim. 1983. A guide to field identification of North American birds. Western Publishing Co. Racine, Wisconsin

Schmidt, K. 1989. Personal communication of results from a final fish survey plus species lists compiled from three surveys since August 1988.

USDA. 1999. The PLANTS database. NPDC, Baton Rouge, Louisiana.

Appendix 1. NPSpecies bibliographic references for PIPE.

Author unknown. 1976. No title. The original citation from NPSpecies = UNKNOWN, 1976.

Becker, D., T. Bragg, and D. Sutherland. 1986. Vegetation survey and prairie management plan for Pipestone NM.

Disrud, D. T. 1966. Plant collections, Pipestone National Monument. Pipestone National Monument, Pipestone, Minnesota.

Fogell, D. 2004. A herpetofaunal inventory of Pipestone National Monument. Technical Report NPS/HTLN/PIPE/CA6000A0100.

Moore, J. W. 1967. Native flowering plants of Pipestone NM. The original citation from NPSpecies = Moore, John W. 1967. Native flowering plants of Pipestone NM.

Moriarty, J. J. 1985. A survey of amphibians and reptiles in the Missouri River drainage of southwestern Minnesota. Minnesota Herpetological Society, Minneapolis.

NPS, Heartland Network. 2006. PIPE herpetofauna inventory geodatabase. Dataset.

Peitz, D. G. 2003. 2003 fish community and Topeka shiner monitoring report. Annual report of activities conducted in 2003 under permits: U.S. Fish and Wildlife Service Subpermit # SP01-07-01 under authority of permits PRT-704930 and PRT-697830 Kansas.

Pietz, D. G. 2002. Fish community and Topeka shiner monitoring for Tallgrass Prairie National Preserve and Pipestone National Monument.

Pietz, D. G. 2002. Fish community and Topeka shiner monitoring for Tallgrass Prairie National Preserve and Pipestone NM.

Powell, A. N. 2000. Grassland bird inventory of seven prairie parks. United States Geological Survey. Wilson's Creek National Battlefield, Missouri.

Schmidt, K. 1989. Results from the final fish survey plus species lists compiled from three surveys since August 1988. Attached to August 18, 1989 letter to Denise Boudreau from Konrad Schmidt.

Snyder, E. J. 1985. Birds of Pipestone National Monument, Pipestone Co, Minnesota. , . ( ). Iowa State University.

Snyder, E. J. 1986. Small mammal habitat use and some population parameters of *Microtus pennsylvanicus* and *Sorex cinereus* at Pipestone National Monument. Iowa State University, Ames, Iowa. Includes maps of study areas, tables and charts. Appendix II & III.

Snyder, E. J. 1986. Small mammal habitat use and some population parametersof *Microtus pennsylvanicus* and *Sorex cinereus* at Pipestone National Monument. Appendix III list of birds.

Appendix 2. NPSpecies Data Dictionary

Park Status	The current status of each species in each park.	Applicable only to organisms with the *Local List* checkbox checked. The possible values reflect a combination of confidence, and availability and currency of verifiable evidence in NPSpecies.
Present in Park	Species' occurrence in park is documented and assumed to be extant.	Extremely high confidence that the species is currently in the park. A current, verifiable reference, voucher, or observation is included in NPSpecies.
Probably Present	Park is within species' range and contains appropriate habitat. Documented occurrences of the species in the adjoining region of the park give reason to suspect that it probably occurs within the park. The degree of probability may vary within this category, including species that range from common to rare.	Very high confidence that the organism is currently in the park. Verifiable evidence may exist in NPSpecies, but is not considered current enough to elevate the status to Present in Park. Efforts should be made to obtain current, verifiable evidence in NPSpecies to elevate the Park Status to "Present in Park". If reasonable efforts to obtain current, verifiable evidence are unsuccessful, then the Park Status should be changed to Unconfirmed, Historic, Encroaching, or False Report as applicable.
Unconfirmed	Included for the park based on weak ("unconfirmed record") or no evidence, giving minimal indication of the species' occurrence in the park.	Any confidence from very low to high that the organism is currently in the park. Verifiable evidence may exist in NPSpecies, but it is not considered sufficient enough to elevate the status to Probably Present, nor current enough to elevate the status to Present. Efforts should be made to obtain current, verifiable evidence in NPSpecies to elevate the Park Status to "Present in Park". If reasonable efforts to obtain current, verifiable evidence are unsuccessful, then the Park Status should be changed to Historic, Encroaching, or False Report as applicable.
Encroaching	The species is not documented in the park, but is documented as being adjacent to the park and has potential to occur in the park.	Extremely low confidence that the organism is currently in the park, but extremely high confidence that the organism is currently adjacent to the park. Verifiable evidence may exist in NPSpecies documenting the occurrence in the park, but it is not current. Potential invasive organisms are good candidates for this Park Status designation, either before they enter a park or after they have been eliminated from a park.
Historic	Species' historical occurrence in the park is documented, but recent investigations indicate that the species is now probably absent.	Extremely low confidence that the organism is currently in the park. Verifiable evidence exists in NPSpecies, but is not current. Extinct, extirpated or eliminated species are candidates for a Historic *Park Status* designation.
False Report	Species previously reported to occur within the park, but current evidence indicates that the report was based on a misidentification, a taxonomic concept no longer accepted, or some other similar problem of interpretation.	Extremely low confidence that the organism is currently in the park. Evidence exists in NPSpecies, but it cannot be sufficiently verified.

Appendix (cont.). NPSpecies Data Dictionary

Abundance	The current abundance of each organism in each park.	Applicable only to organisms with the *Local List* checkbox checked and a *Park Status* of "Present". The values attempt to balance abundance with suitable habitat, and temporal/behavioral considerations. In practice, the entered value should apply (although there are numerous exceptions) to the abundance in the most suitable habitat of the organism, and at the time that the organism is engaged in it's principle behavior in (e.g. breeding, migrating, hibernating, etc.), or most important behavior to, the park. A future generation of NPSpecies will address the coding of *Abundance* (and associated *Residency*) to separate out the temporal and behavioral aspects. The Data Source field for Abundance is available to provide a citation that specifically addresses abundance in more detail.
Abundant		**Animals:** May be seen daily, in suitable habitat and season, and counted in relatively large numbers. **Plants:** Large number of individuals; wide ecological amplitude or occurring in habitats covering a large portion of the park.
Common		**Animals:** May be seen daily, in suitable habitat and season, but not in large numbers. **Plants:** Large numbers of individuals predictably occurring in commonly encountered habitats but not those covering a large portion of the
Uncommon		**Animals:** Likely to be seen monthly in appropriate season/habitat. May be locally common. **Plants:** Few to moderate numbers of individuals; occurring either sporadically in commonly encountered habitats or in uncommon habitats.
Rare		**Animals:** Present, but usually seen only a few times each year. **Plants:** Few individuals usually restricted to small areas of rare habitat.
Occasional		**Animals:** Occurs in the park at least once every few years, but not necessarily every year. **Plants:** Not applicable.
Unknown		Abundance unknown.

Residency	Current residency classification for each ANIMAL species in each park.	Applicable only to ANIMALS with the *Local List* checkbox checked and a *Park Status* of "Present". The values attempt to balance temporal and behavioral considerations. In practice, the entered value should apply (although there are numerous exceptions) to the residency of the organism at the time that the organism is engaged in its principle behavior (e.g. breeding, migrating, hibernating, etc.) in, or most important behavior to, the park. A future generation of NPSpecies will address the coding of Residency (and associated Abundance) to separate out the temporal and behavior aspects. The Data Source field for Residency is available to provide a citation that specifically addresses Residency in more detail.
Breeder		Population reproduces in the park.
Resident		A significant population is maintained in the park for more than two months each year, but it is not known to breed there.
Migratory		Migratory species that occurs in park approximately two months or less each year and does not breed there.
Vagrant		Park is outside of the species' usual range.
Unknown		Residency status in park is unknown.

Appendix (cont.). NPSpecies Data Dictionary

Nativity	Nativity classification for each organism for each park	Applicable only to organisms with the *Local List* checkbox checked. If the park-status of an organism is not "Present in Park", then nativity represents the nativity if the organism were eventually confirmed in the park.
	Native	Native The organism is native, or would be native, to the park (either endemic or indigenous).
	Non-native	The organism is not native, or would not be native, to the park (neither endemic nor indigenous).
	Unknown	Nativity status in the park is unknown.

The NPS has organized its parks with significant natural resources into 32 networks linked by geography and shared natural resource characteristics. The Heartland Network is composed of 15 National Park Service (NPS) units in eight Midwestern states. These parks contain a wide variety of natural and cultural resources including sites focused on commemorating civil war battlefields, Native American heritage, westward expansion, and our U.S. Presidents. The Network is charged with creating inventories of its species and natural features as well as monitoring trends and issues in order to make sound management decisions. Critical inventories help park managers understand the natural resources in their care while monitoring programs help them understand meaningful change in natural systems and to respond accordingly. The Heartland Network helps to link natural and cultural resources by protecting the habitat of our history.

The I&M program bridges the gap between science and management with a third of its efforts aimed at making information accessible. Each network of parks, such as Heartland, has its own multi-disciplinary team of scientists, support personnel, and seasonal field technicians whose system of online databases and reports make information and research results available to all. Greater efficiency is achieved through shared staff and funding as these core groups of professionals augment work done by individual park staff. Through this type of integration and partnership, network parks are able to accomplish more than a single park could on its own.

The mission of the Heartland Network is to collaboratively develop and conduct scientifically credible inventories and long-term monitoring of park "vital signs" and to distribute this information for use by park staff, partners, and the public, thus enhancing understanding which leads to sound decision making in the preservation of natural resources and cultural history held in trust by the National Park Service.

www.nature.nps.gov/im/units/htln/

Natural Resource Monitoring

The Department of the Interior protects and manages the nation's natural resources and cultural heritage; provides scientific and other information about those resources; and honors its special responsibilities to American Indians, Alaska Natives, and affiliated Island Communities.

NPS D-XXX, Month Year

www.ingramcontent.com/pod-product-compliance
Lightning Source LLC
Chambersburg PA
CBHW080936290526
45795CB00007BA/2774